all-time hit songs *arranged for* ukulele

This publication is not authorised for sale in the United States of America and/or Canada

Wise Publications
part of The Music Sales Group
London/New York/Paris/Sydney/Copenhagen/Berlin/Madrid/Tokyo

Published by:
Wise Publications,
14-15 Berners Street, London W1T 3LJ, UK.

Exclusive Distributors:
Music Sales Limited,
Distribution Centre, Newmarket Road, Bury St Edmunds,
Suffolk IP33 3YB, UK.
Music Sales Pty Limited,
20 Resolution Drive, Caringbah, NSW 2229, Australia.

Order No. AM995082
ISBN 978-1-84772-681-0

Edited by David Harrison.
Cover designed by Fresh Lemon.
Photographs courtesy of Matthew Ward.

Printed in the EU.

Your Guarantee of Quality
As publishers, we strive to produce every book to the highest commercial standards.

The music has been freshly engraved and the book has been carefully designed to minimise awkward page turns and to make playing from it a real pleasure.

Particular care has been given to specifying acid-free, neutral-sized paper made from pulps which have not been elemental chlorine bleached.

This pulp is from farmed sustainable forests and was produced with special regard for the environment.

Throughout, the printing and binding have been planned to ensure a sturdy, attractive publication which should give years of enjoyment.

If your copy fails to meet our high standards, please inform us and we will gladly replace it.

www.musicsales.com

...baby one more time

Words & Music by Max Martin

N.C.

Oh ba-by, ba-by. Oh ba-by, ba-by.

Cm G7 B♭

1. Oh ba - by, ba - by how was I sup - posed to know
2. Oh ba - by, ba - by the rea - son I breath is you

E♭ (3fr) Fm G7 Cm

that some - thin' was - n't right here?
boy you got me blind - ed.

G7 B♭

Oh ba - by, ba - by I should - n't have let you go.
Oh pret - ty ba - by There's no - thing that I would - n'y do.

E♭ (3fr) Fm G7 Cm

And now you're out of sight yeah.
It's not the way I planned it.

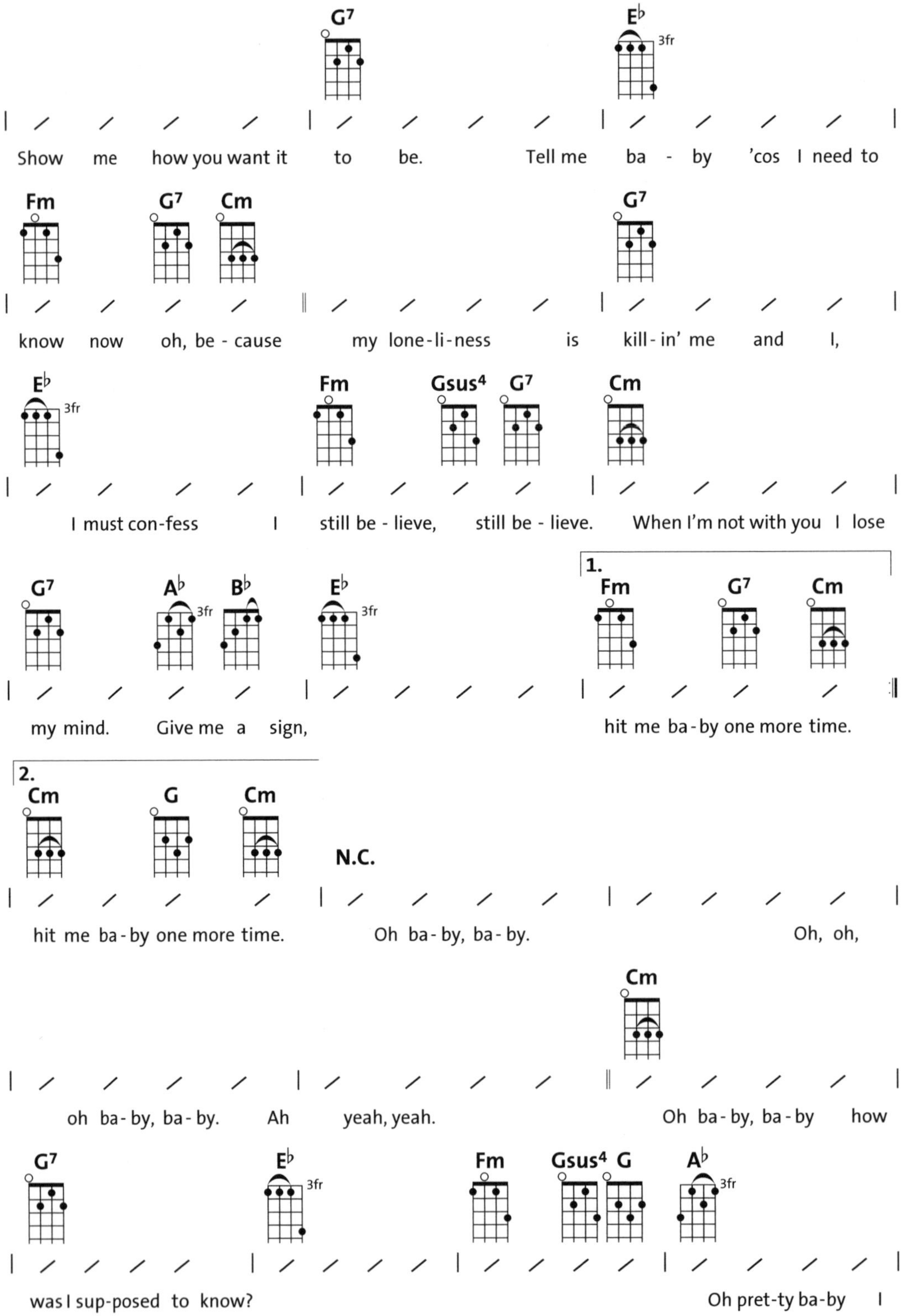
G7
E♭
3fr
Show me how you want it to be. Tell me ba - by 'cos I need to
Fm G7 Cm
G7
know now oh, be - cause my lone-li-ness is kill-in' me and I,
E♭
3fr
Fm Gsus4 G7 Cm
I must con-fess I still be - lieve, still be - lieve. When I'm not with you I lose
G7 A♭ B♭ E♭
3fr
1.
Fm G7 Cm
my mind. Give me a sign, hit me ba-by one more time.
2.
Cm G Cm
N.C.
hit me ba-by one more time. Oh ba-by, ba-by. Oh, oh,
Cm
oh ba-by, ba-by. Ah yeah, yeah. Oh ba-by, ba-by how
G7
E♭
Fm Gsus4 G
A♭
was I sup-posed to know? Oh pret-ty ba-by I

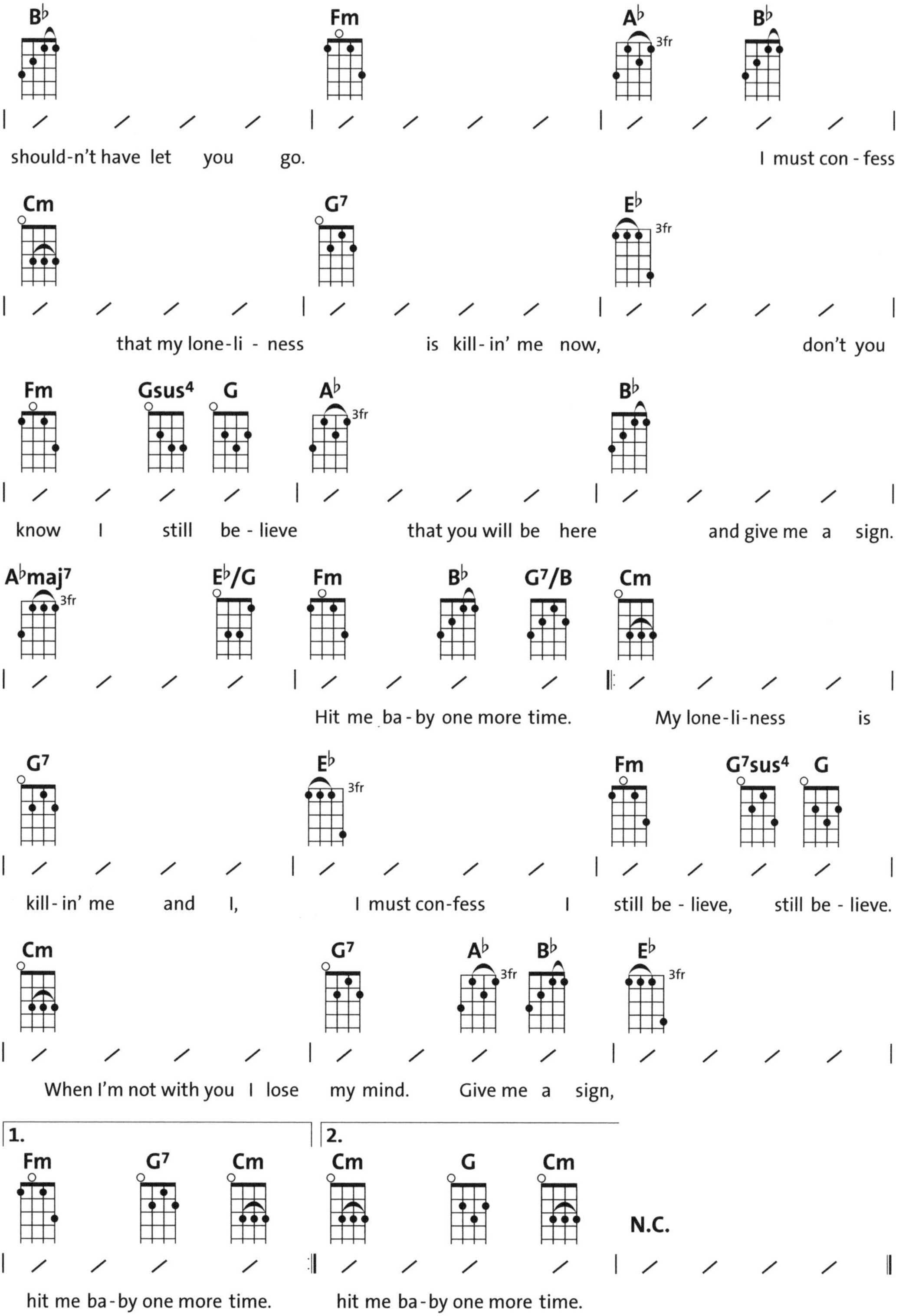
B♭ Fm A♭ 3fr B♭
should-n't have let you go. I must con-fess
Cm G7 E♭ 3fr
that my lone-li - ness is kill-in' me now, don't you
Fm Gsus4 G A♭ 3fr B♭
know I still be - lieve that you will be here and give me a sign.
A♭maj7 3fr E♭/G Fm B♭ G7/B Cm
Hit me ba - by one more time. My lone-li-ness is
G7 E♭ 3fr Fm G7sus4 G
kill-in' me and I, I must con-fess I still be - lieve, still be - lieve.
Cm G7 A♭ 3fr B♭ E♭ 3fr
When I'm not with you I lose my mind. Give me a sign,
1. Fm G7 Cm
hit me ba-by one more time.
2. Cm G Cm N.C.
hit me ba-by one more time.

big spender

Words by Dorothy Fields
Music by Cy Coleman

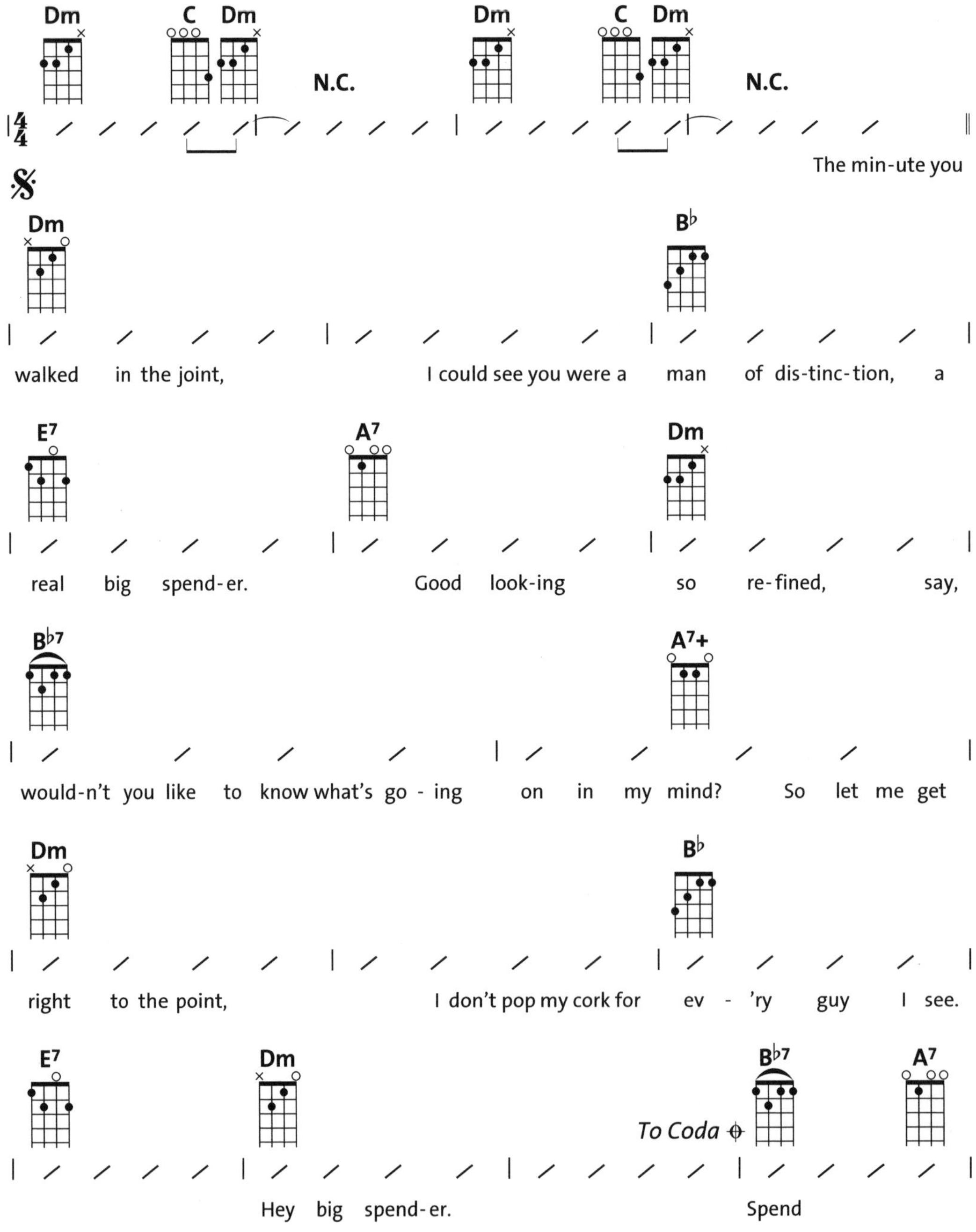

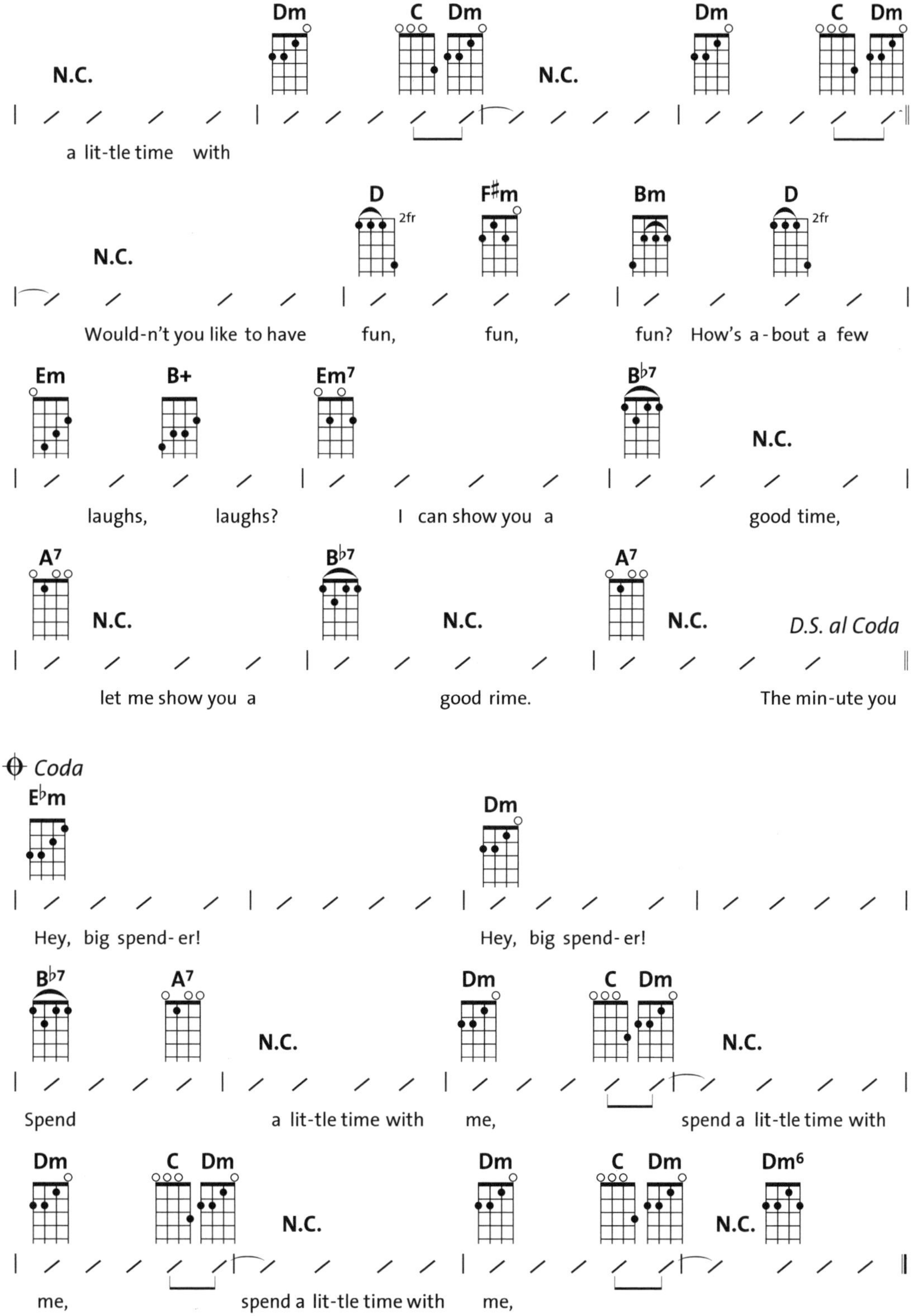
Dm C Dm Dm C Dm
N.C. N.C.
a lit-tle time with
D F♯m Bm D
2fr 2fr
N.C.
Would-n't you like to have fun, fun, fun? How's a-bout a few
Em B+ Em7 B♭7
N.C.
laughs, laughs? I can show you a good time,
A7 B♭7 A7
N.C. N.C. N.C.
D.S. al Coda
let me show you a good rime. The min-ute you
Coda
E♭m Dm
Hey, big spend-er! Hey, big spend-er!
B♭7 A7 Dm C Dm
N.C. N.C.
Spend a lit-tle time with me, spend a lit-tle time with
Dm C Dm Dm C Dm Dm6
N.C. N.C.
me, spend a lit-tle time with me,

the girl from ipanema

Music by Antonio Carlos Jobim
English Words by Norman Gimbel
Original Words Vinicius De Moraes

Fmaj7

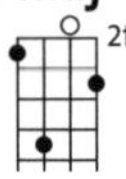

Tall and tan and young and {love - ly, the girl / hand - some, the boy}

G7

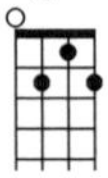

from I - pa - ne - ma goes walk - ing, and when

Gm7

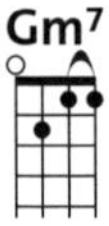

G♭7

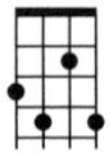

she {pass - es, each one / he {pass - es, each girl} she / he} pass - es goes

Fmaj7

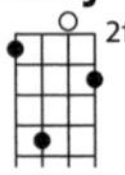

G♭7

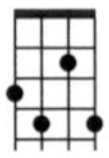

Fmaj7

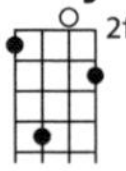

"aah!" When {she walks she's / he walks he's} like

G7

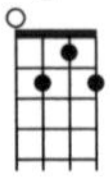

a sam - ba that swings so cool and sways so gen - tle, that when

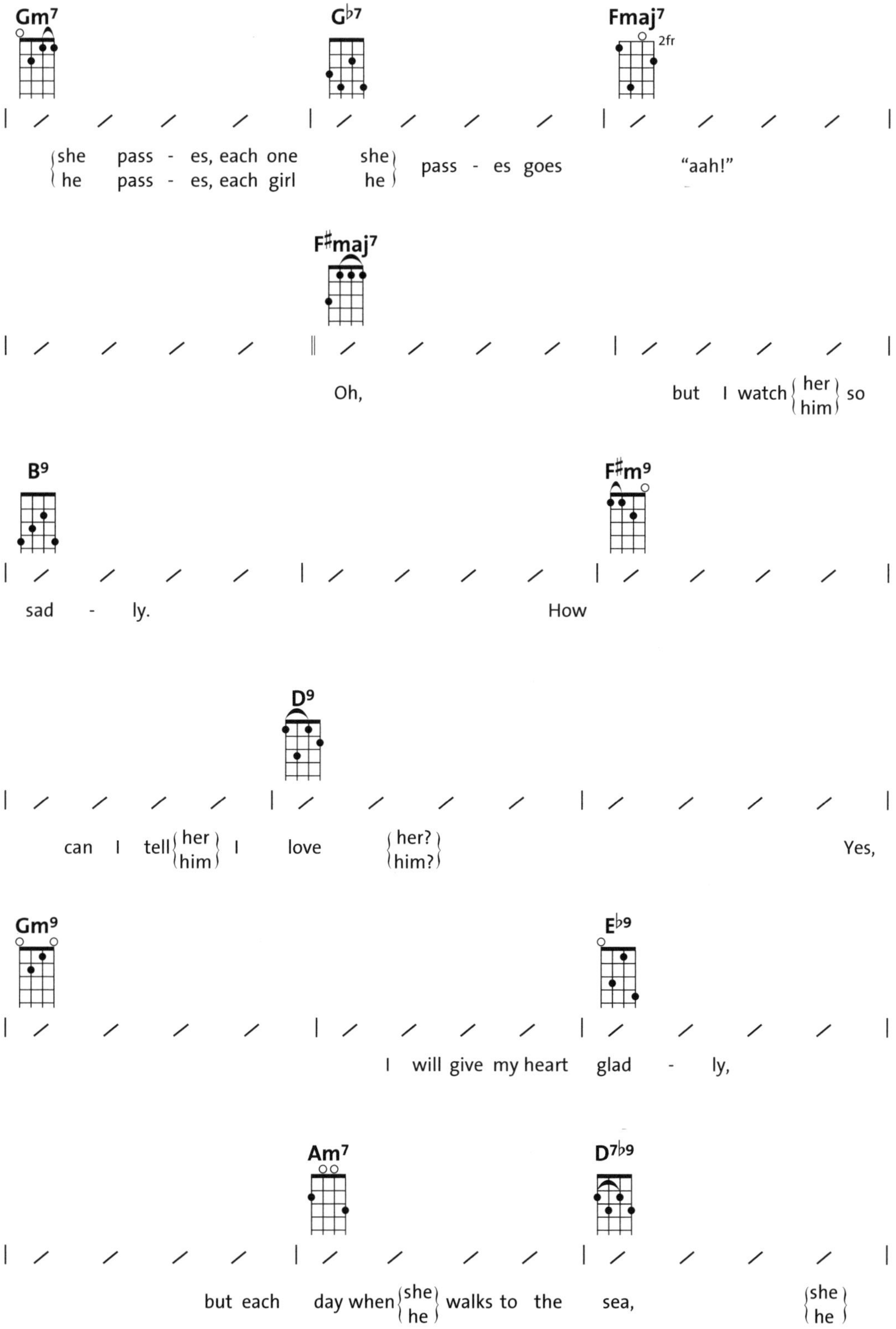
Gm7
G♭7
Fmaj7
2fr
{she pass - es, each one she} pass - es goes "aah!"
{he pass - es, each girl he}
F♯maj7
Oh, but I watch {her / him} so
B9
F♯m9
sad - ly. How
D9
can I tell {her / him} I love {her? / him?} Yes,
Gm9
E♭9
I will give my heart glad - ly,
Am7
D7♭9
but each day when {she / he} walks to the sea, {she / he}

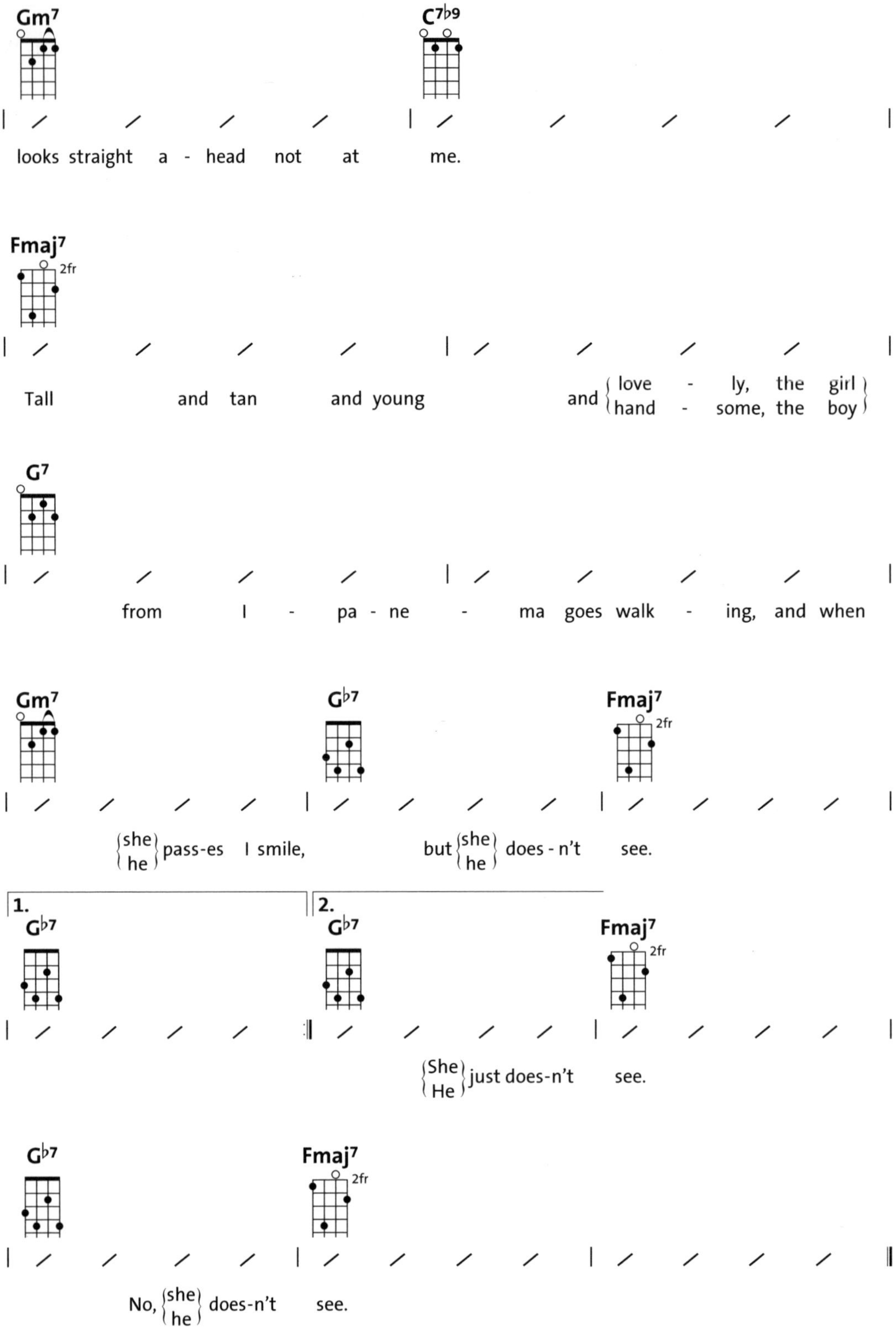
Gm7
C7♭9
looks straight a - head not at me.
Fmaj7
2fr
Tall and tan and young and {love - ly, the girl / hand - some, the boy}
G7
from I - pa - ne - ma goes walk - ing, and when
Gm7
G♭7
Fmaj7
2fr
{she / he} pass-es I smile, but {she / he} does - n't see.
1.
G♭7
2.
G♭7
Fmaj7
2fr
{She / He} just does-n't see.
G♭7
Fmaj7
2fr
No, {she / he} does-n't see.

going underground

Words & Music by Paul Weller

D5 D6 D5

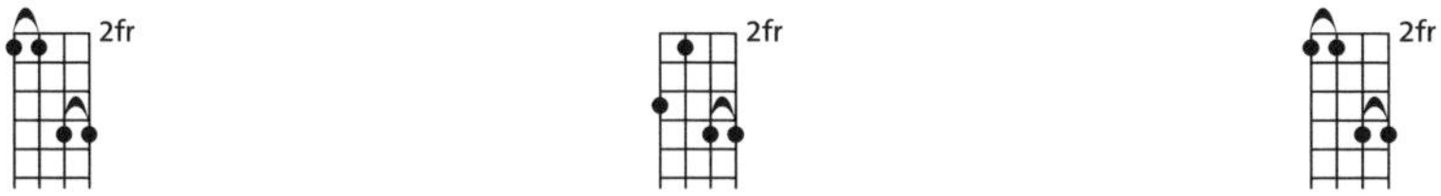

4/4

1. Some peo-ple might say my life is in a rut, I'm quite
2. Some peo-ple might get some plea-sure out of hate. Me I've e -

D6 D5 D6

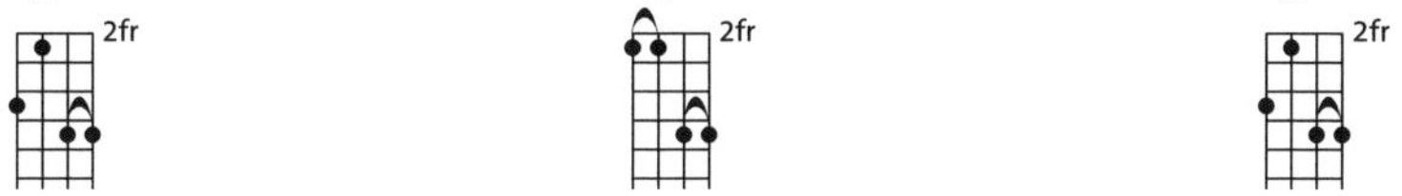

hap - py with what I've got. Peo-ple might say that I should strive for
-nough al - ready on my plate. Peo-ple might need some ten-sion to re -

D5 D6

more. But I'm so hap - py, I can't see the (point).
- lax. Me, I'm too bu - sy dodg - in' 'tween the (flak)

B D♯m B

Some-thing's hap-pen-ing here to - day, a show of strength with your
What you see is what you get, you made your bed you bet-ter

D♯m B D♯m

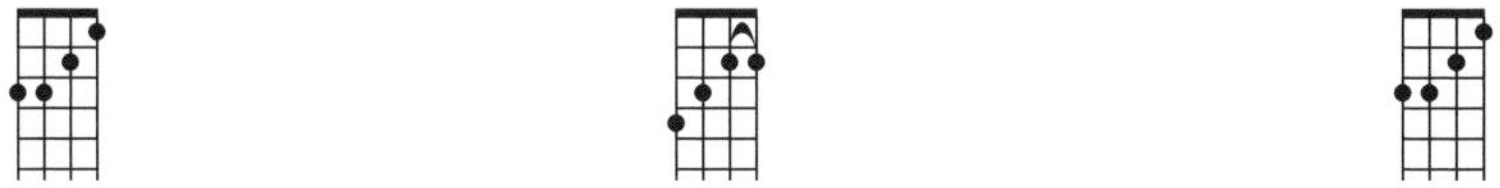

boy's bri - gade. And I'm so hap-py and you're so kind, you
lie in it. You choose your lead-ers and place your trust, their

B **D♯m**

| / / / / | / / / / |

want more mon - ey of course I don't mind. To
lies wash you down and their pro - mi - ses rust. You'll see

E **F♯**

| / / / / | / / / / |

buy nuc - lear text - books for a - tom - ic crimes and the
kid - ney ma - chines re - placed by rock - ets and guns, the

B **D♯m**

| / / / / | / / / / |

pub - lic gets what the pub - lic wants, but
pub - lic wants what the pub - lic gets, but

E **F♯**

| / / / / | / / / / ||

I want no - thing this so - ci - e - ty's got.
I don't care what this so - ci - e - ty wants.
I'm go - ing

B **D♯m** **E**

| / / / / | / / / / | / / / / |

un - der - ground. (Go - ing un - der - ground.) Well, let the brass band play and feet

F♯ **B** **D♯m**

| / / / / | / / / / | / / / / |

start to pound. Go - ing un - der - ground. (Go - ing un - der - ground.) Well, let the

E | **F♯**

| / / / / | / / / / |

boys all sing and let the boys all shout for to -

1.

B | **D♯m** | **E** | **F♯**

| / / / / | / / / / | / / / / | / / / / :||

- mor- row.

2.

C♯m **C♯m7** **C♯m** | **B** | **C♯m** **C♯m7** **C♯m** | **B**

| / / / / | / / / / | / / / / | / / / / |

- mor - row. Ho! La, la, la, la. (Ho!) La, la, la, la. We

C♯m | **B** | **C♯m**

| / / / / | / / / / | / / / / |

talk and we talk un - til my head ex - plodes, I turn on the news and my

B | **D♯m** | **E**

| / / / / | / / / / | / / / / |

bo - dy froze. The bray-ing sheep on my T. V. screen make

F♯ | | **D♭**

| / / / / | / / / / || / / / / |

this boy shout, make this boy scream. Go - ing un - der - ground.

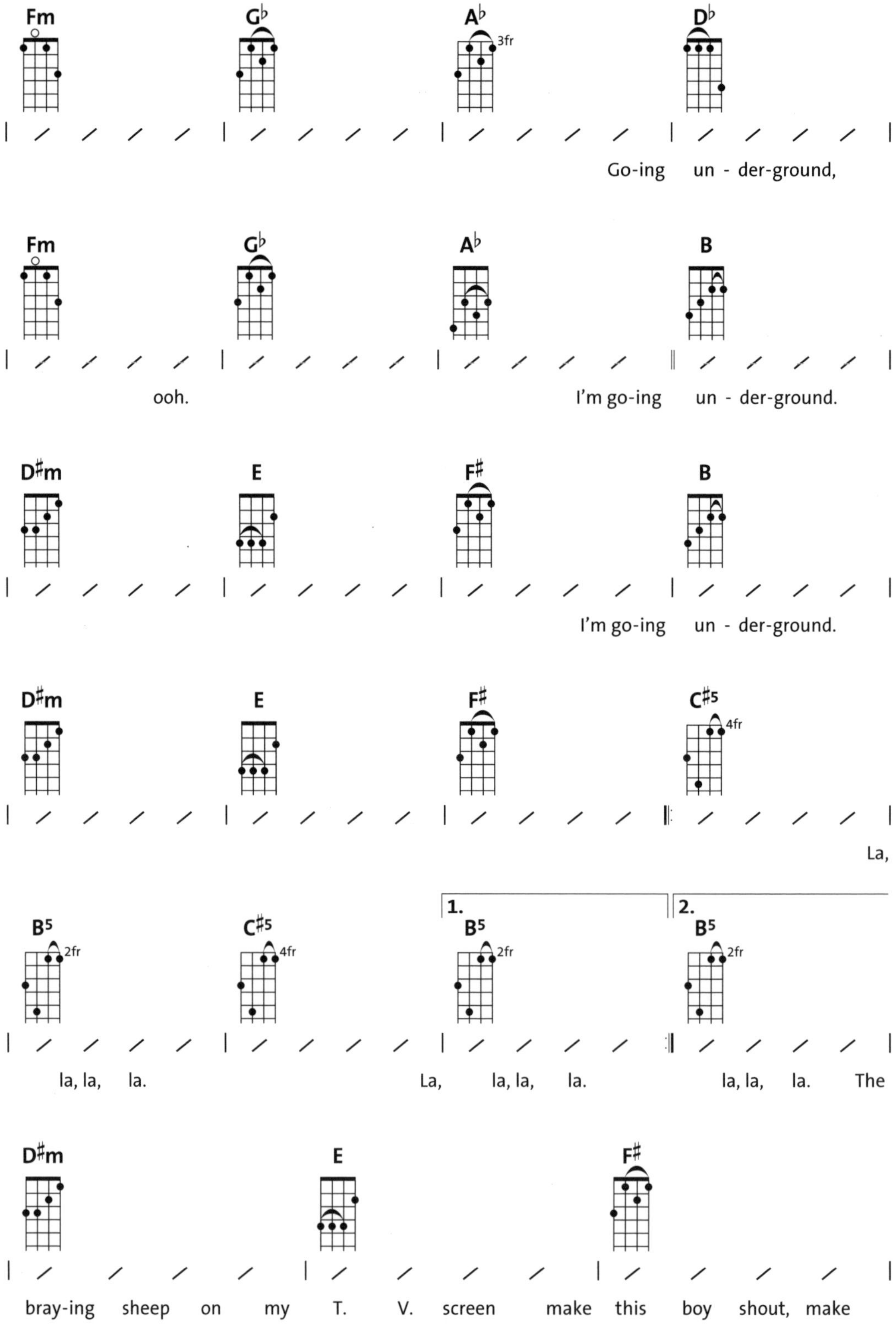
Fm G♭ A♭ D♭
3fr
Go-ing un - der-ground,
Fm G♭ A♭ B
ooh. I'm go-ing un - der-ground.
D♯m E F♯ B
I'm go-ing un - der-ground.
D♯m E F♯ C♯5
4fr
La,
1. 2.
B5 C♯5 B5 B5
2fr 4fr 2fr 2fr
la, la, la. La, la, la, la. la, la, la. The
D♯m E F♯
bray-ing sheep on my T. V. screen make this boy shout, make

D♭ 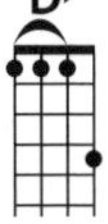 Fm 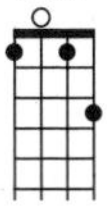

this boy scream. Go-ing ‖ un - der - ground. (Go - ing | un - der- ground.) Well, let the

G♭ 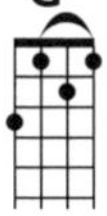 A♭ 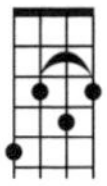 D♭ 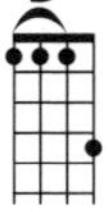

brass band play and feet | start to pound. Go - ing | un - der - ground. (Go - ing

Fm 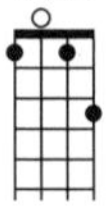 G♭ 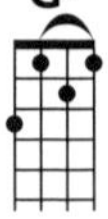 A♭ 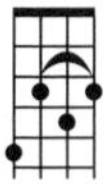

un - der- ground.) Well, let the | boys all sing and let the | boys all shout. Go - ing

D♭ 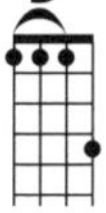 Fm 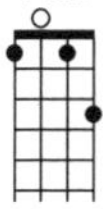 G♭ 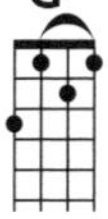

un - der - ground. (Go - ing | un - der- ground.) Well, let the | brass band play and feet go

A♭ 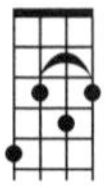 D♭ 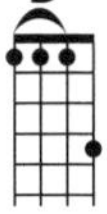 Fm 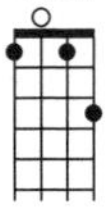

pow, pow, pow. Go-ing | un - der - ground. (Go - ing | un - der- ground.) So let the

G♭ 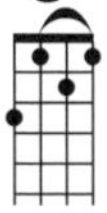 A♭ 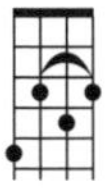 G♭6 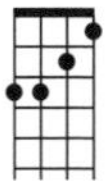

boys all sing and let the | boys all shout for to - | mor- row, oh.

hallelujah i love her so

Words & Music by Ray Charles

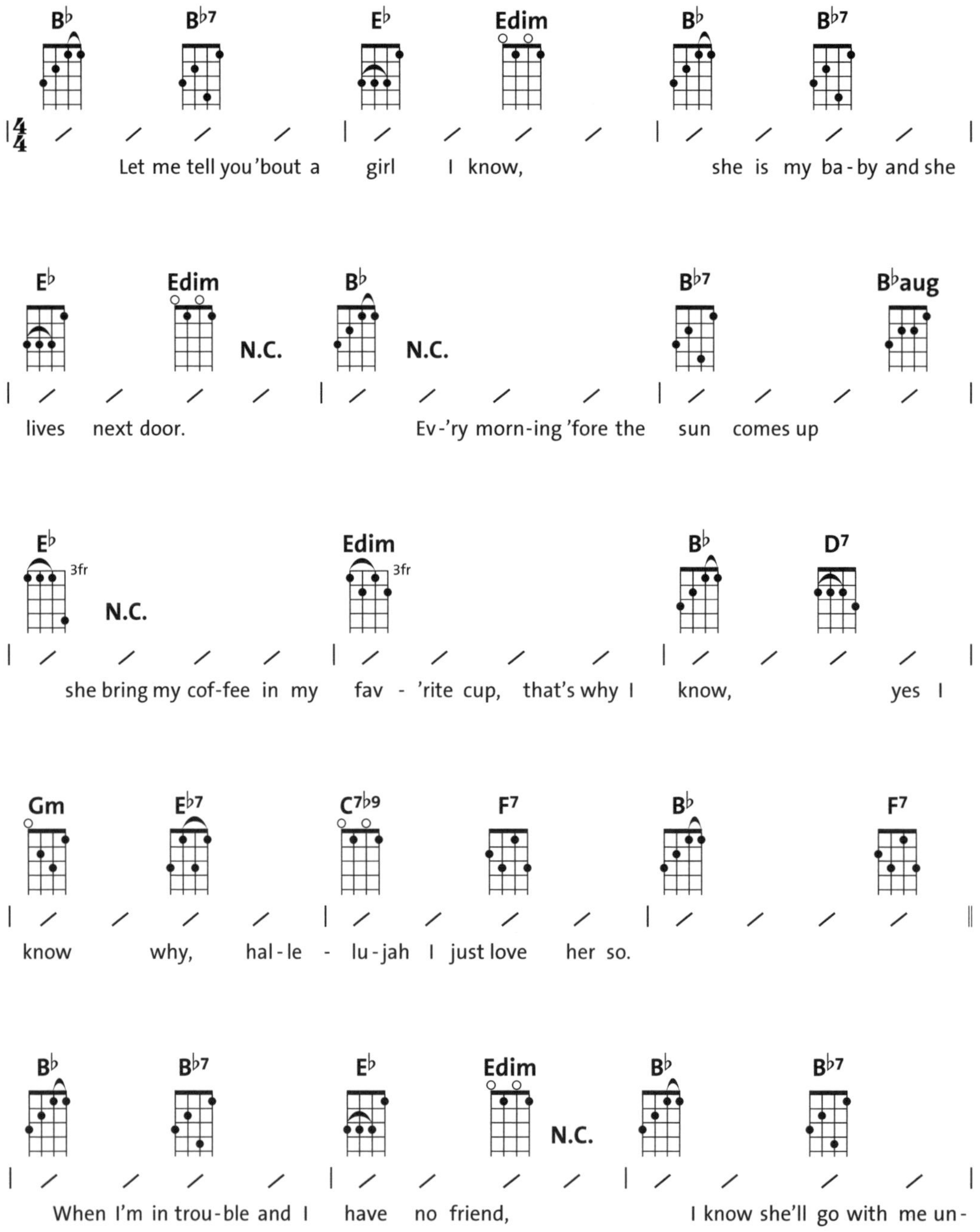

E♭ Edim N.C. B♭ N.C. B♭7 B♭aug

til the end. Ev-'ry-bo-dy asks my how I know,

E♭ (3fr) N.C. Edim (3fr) N.C. B♭ D7

I smile at them and say she told me so. That's why I know, oh

Gm E♭7 C7♭9 F7 B♭ B♭aug

I know, hal-le-lu-jah I just love her so.

E♭ N.C. Edim B♭ N.C.

Now if I call her on the te-le-phone, and tell her that I'm

B♭7 E7 E♭7 N.C.

all a-lone, by the time I count from

D♭7 C7 N.C. F7

one to four, I hear her on my door.

B♭ B♭7 E♭ Edim

In the eve - ning when the sun go down,

B♭ B♭7 E♭ Edim

when there is no - bo - dy else a - round,

B♭ N.C. B♭7 B♭aug E♭ (3fr) N.C.

she kiss-es me and she hold me tight, and tell me Dad-dy ev-'ry -

Edim (3fr) N.C. B♭ D7 Gm E♭7

- thing's all right. That's why I know, yes I know, hal - le -

C7♭9 F7 B♭ Gm C7 F7

- lu - jah I just love her so. Oh, hal - le - lu - jah,

B♭ Gm C7 F7

don't you know I just love her so.

Repeat to fade

homeward bound

Words & Music by Paul Simon

C F C

4/4

1. I'm

C

(1.) sit - tin' in the rail - way sta - tion, got a
2. Ev - 'ry day's an end - less stream of
(3.) night I'll sing my song a - gain, I'll

Em

tick - et for my des - ti - na - tion.
cig - a - rettes and ma - ga - zines.
play the game and pre - tend.

Gm6 A7

Mm.
Mm. And
Mm. But

Dm

On a tour of one night stands, my
each town looks the same to me, the
all my words come back to me in

B♭

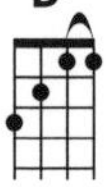

suit - case and gui - tar in hand_ and
mov - ies and the fac - tor - ies and
shades of me - di - oc - ri - ty like

C

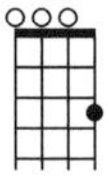

ev - 'ry stop is neat - ly planned for a
ev - 'ry strang - er's face I re -
emp - ti - ness in har - mo - ny I

G7 C

 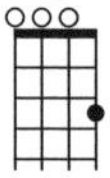

po - et and a one man band.
minds me that I long to be,
need some - one to com - fort me.

C F C

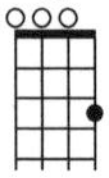 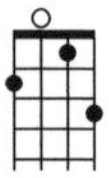 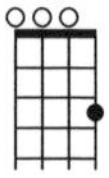

Home - ward bound, I wish I was,

F

home - ward bound.

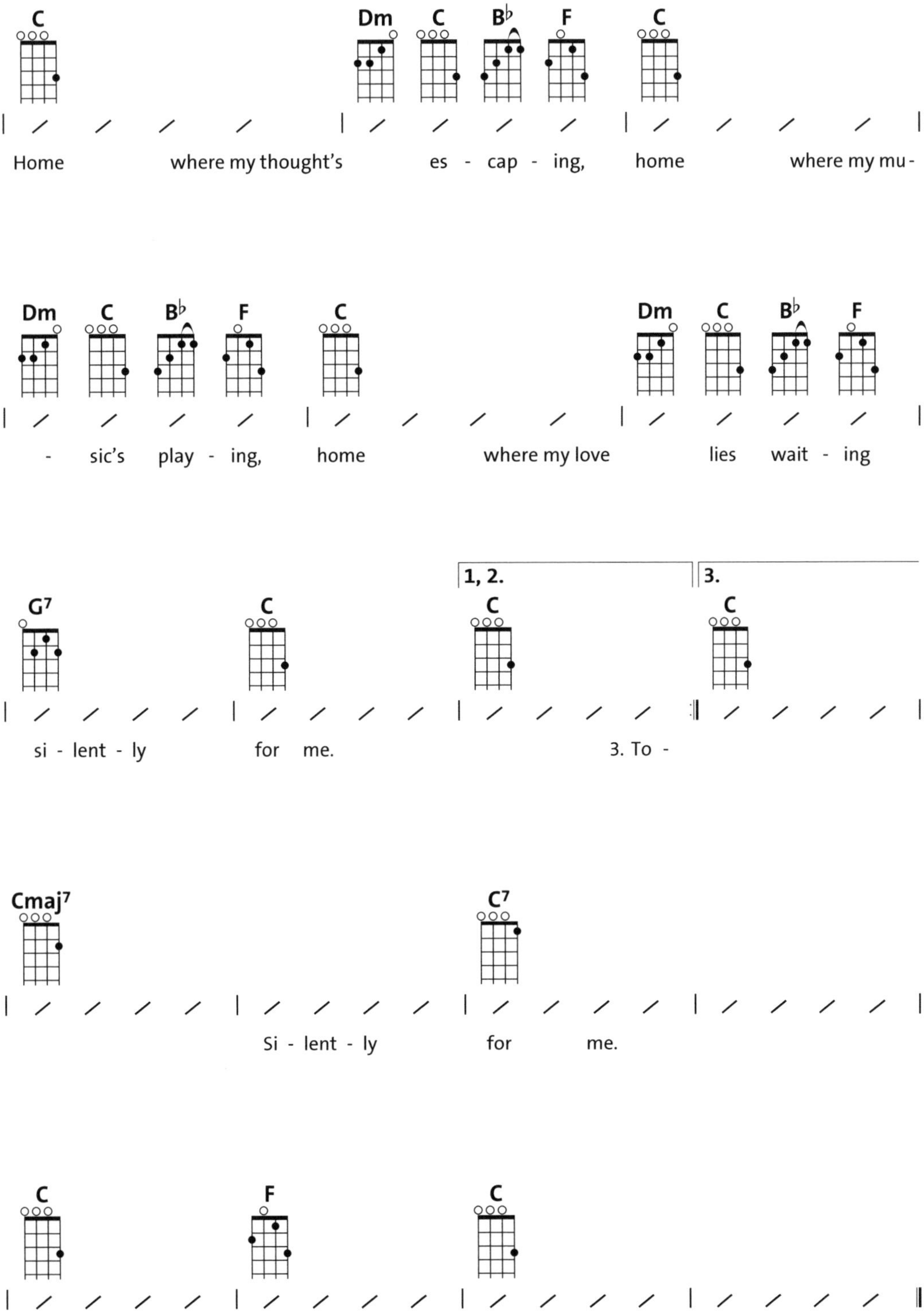
C Dm C B♭ F C
Home where my thought's es - cap - ing, home where my mu -
Dm C B♭ F C Dm C B♭ F
- sic's play - ing, home where my love lies wait - ing
1, 2.
3.
G7 C C C
si - lent - ly for me.
3. To -
Cmaj7 C7
Si - lent - ly for me.
C F C

imagine

Words & Music by John Lennon

C | F | C

4/4 | / / / / | / / / / | / / / / |

1. I - ma-gine there's no hea-ven, it's ea-sy if you try.
2. I - ma-gine there's no coun - tries it is-n't hard to do.

F | C | F

| / / / / | / / / / | / / / / |

No hell be-low us
No-thing to kill or die for

C | F | Am | Dm7 F

| / / / / | / / / / | / / / / | / / / / |

a-bove us on - ly sky. I-ma-gine all the peo - ple,
and no re-li - gion too. I-ma-gine all the peo - ple,

1. G | G7 || 2. G | G7

| / / / / | / / / / :|| / / / / | / / / / |

liv-ing for to day. Ah ah ah. liv-ing life in peace.

F G | C E7 | F G | C E7

| / / / / | / / / / | / / / / | / / / / |

You may say I'm a dream-er, but I'm not the on-ly one.

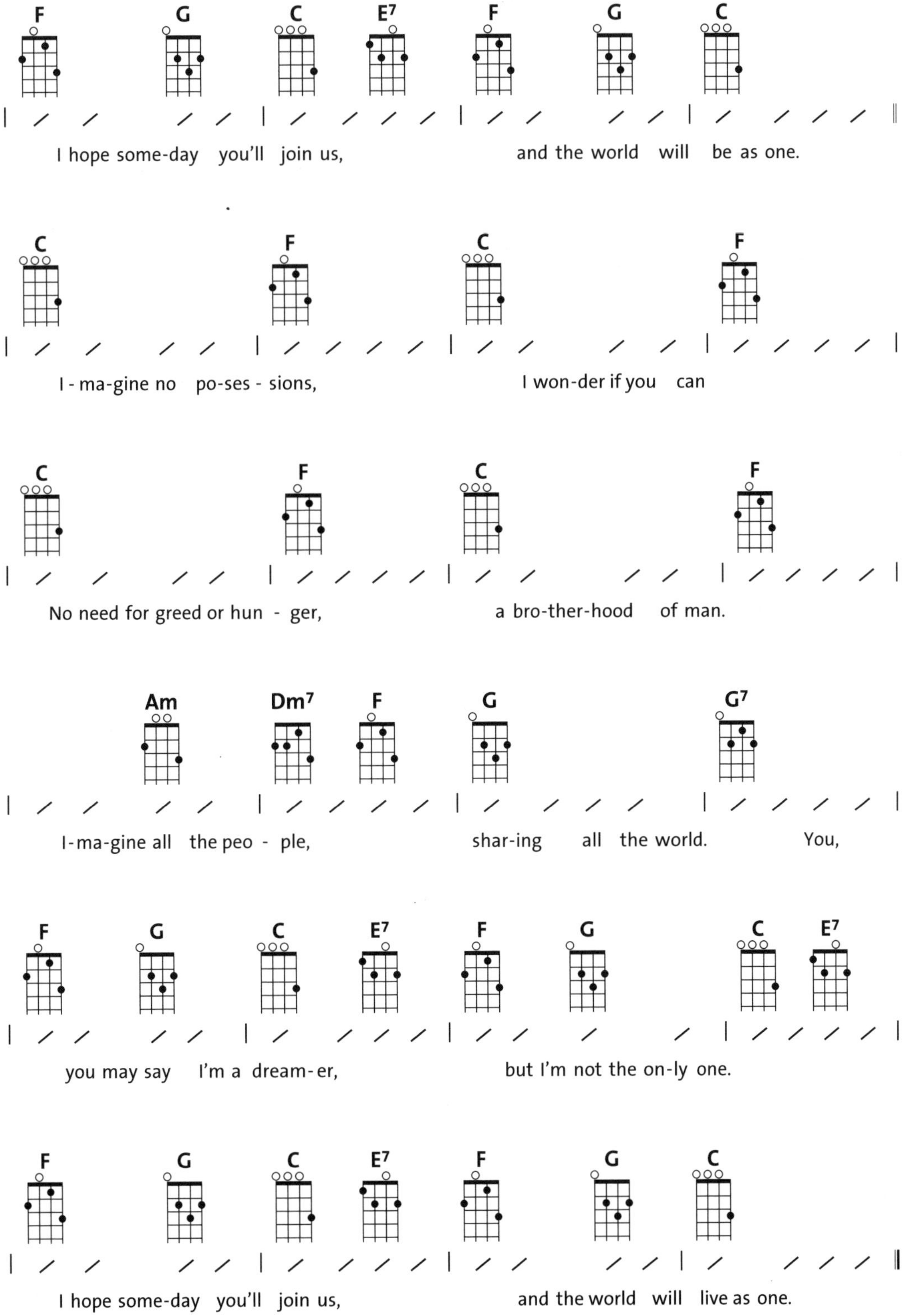
F G C E7 F G C
I hope some-day you'll join us, and the world will be as one.
C F C F
I - ma-gine no po-ses - sions, I won-der if you can
C F C F
No need for greed or hun - ger, a bro-ther-hood of man.
Am Dm7 F G G7
I-ma-gine all the peo - ple, shar-ing all the world. You,
F G C E7 F G C E7
you may say I'm a dream-er, but I'm not the on-ly one.
F G C E7 F G C
I hope some-day you'll join us, and the world will live as one.

jambalaya (on the bayou)

Words & Music by Hank Williams

C G

1. Good - bye Joe, me got-ta go me oh my oh.
(2.) daux, Fon - tain - eaux, the place is buzz - in'.

Me got-ta go pole the pi - rogue down the
Kin - folk come to see Y - vonne by the

C

bay - ou. My Y -
do - zen. Dress in

G

vonne, the sweet - est one, me oh my oh.
style and go hog - wild, me oh my oh.

Son of a gun, we'll have big
Son of a gun, we'll have big

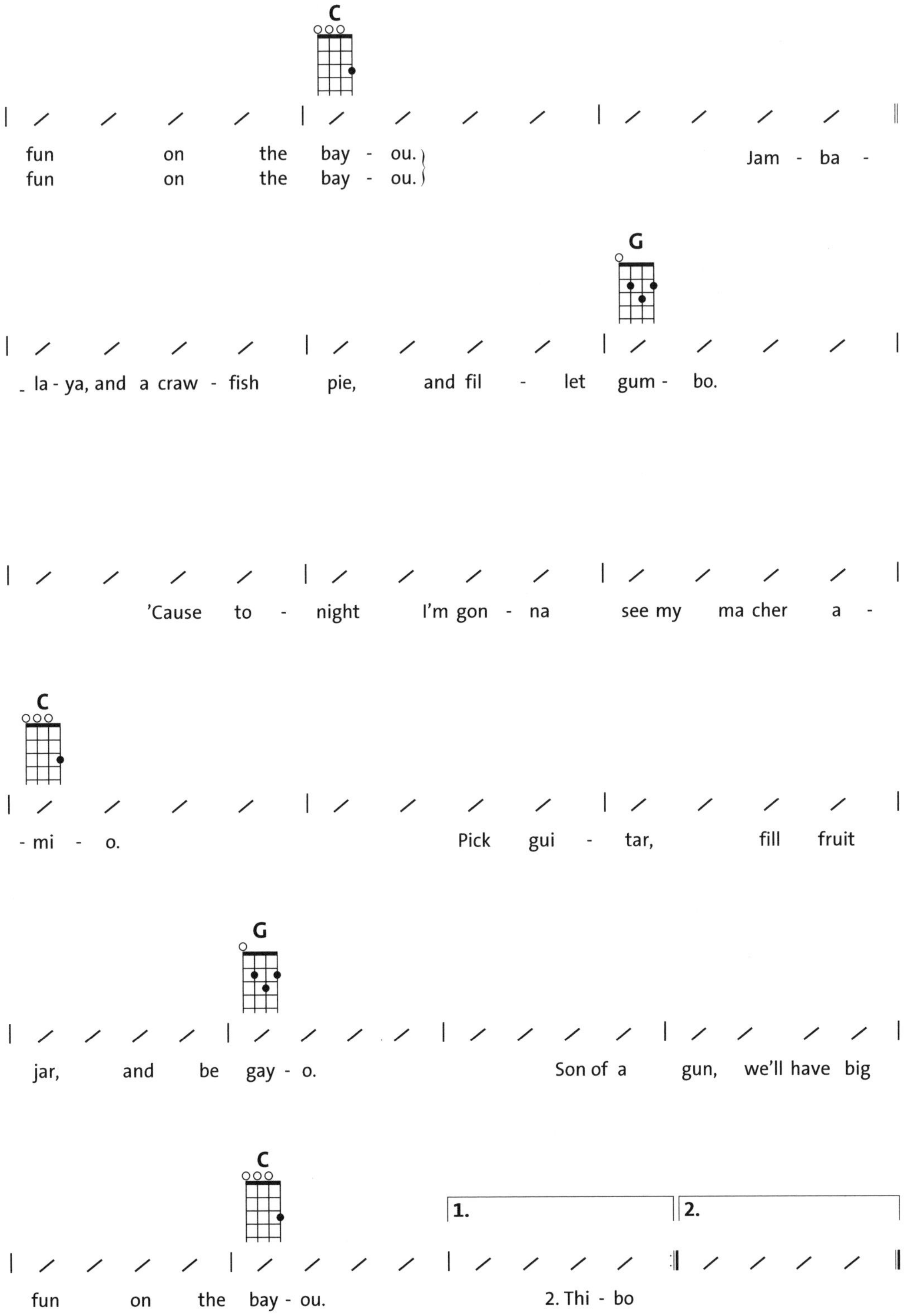
C
fun on the bay - ou.
fun on the bay - ou.
Jam - ba -
G
la - ya, and a craw - fish pie, and fil - let gum - bo.
'Cause to - night I'm gon - na see my ma cher a -
C
- mi - o.
Pick gui - tar, fill fruit
G
jar, and be gay - o.
Son of a gun, we'll have big
C
1.
2.
fun on the bay - ou.
2. Thi - bo

knockin' on heaven's door

Words & Music by Bob Dylan

G D Am⁷

1. Ma - ma, take this badge off of me,
2. Ma - ma, put my guns in the ground,

G D C

I can't use it an - y - more.
I can't shoot them an - y - more.

G D Am⁷

It's get - tin' dark, too dark for me to see,
That long black cloud is com - in' down,

G D C

I feel like I'm knock - in' on hea - ven's door.
I feel like I'm knock - in' on hea - ven's door.

Knock, knock, knock- in' on heav-ven's door.

Knock, knock, knock- in' on hea-ven's door.

Knock, knock, knock- in' on hea-ven's door.

Knock, knock, knock- in' on hea-ven's door.

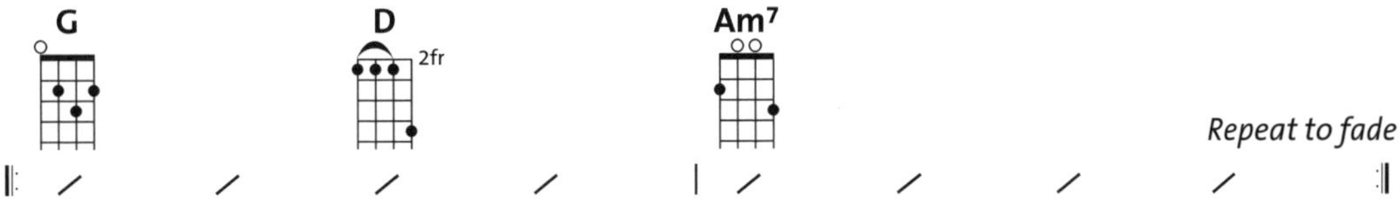

Repeat to fade

la vie en rose

Words by Edith Piaf
Music by R.S. Louiguy

Quand il me prend dans ses bras, il me par - le tout
Hold me close and hold me fast, the ma - gic spell you

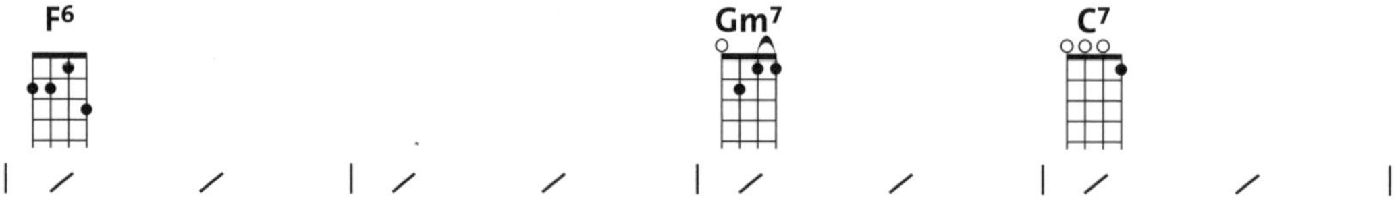

bas, je vois la vie en ro - se.
cast, this is la vie en ro - se.

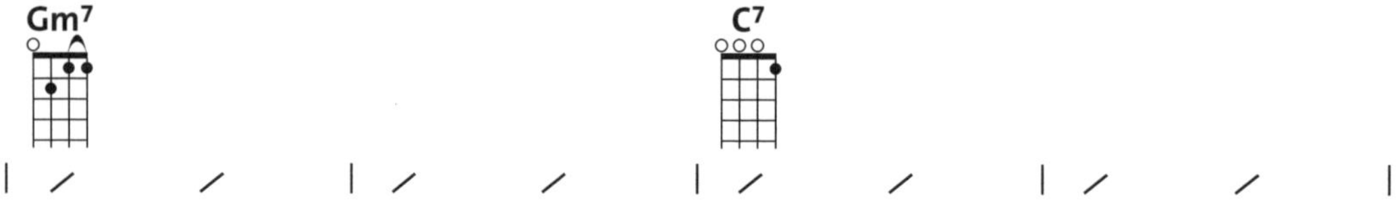

Il me dit des mots d'a - mour, des mots de tous les
When you kiss me hea - ven sighs, and though I close my

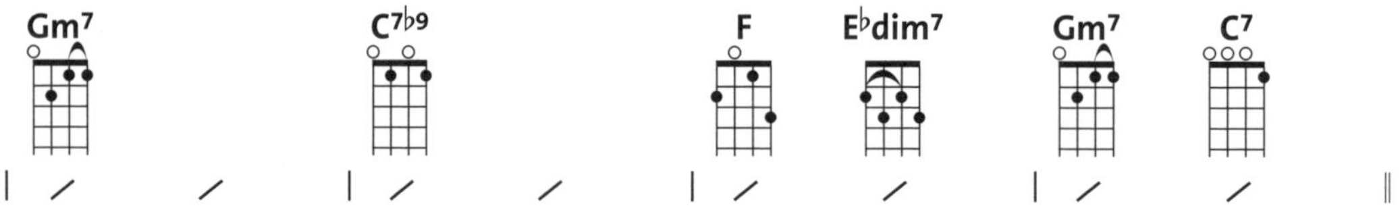

jours, et ça m'fait quel - que cho - se.
eyes, I see la - vie en ro - se.

Il est en - tré dans mon cœur, un - e part de bon -
When you press me to your heart. I'm in a world a -

F6 F7 B♭

heur dont je con - nais la cau - se.
part a world where ro - ses bloom.

B♭m Am7 Dm

C'est lui pour moi, moi pour lui dans la vie,
And when you speak an - gels sing from a - bove,

rit.

G7 Gm7 B♭m C7♭9

Il me la dit, l'a ju - ré pour la vi - e.
ev - 'ry-day words seem to turn in - to love songs.

a tempo

F Fmaj7

Et dès que je l'a - per - çois a - lors je sens en
Give your heart and soul to me and life will al - ways

F6 Gm7 C7 D♭maj7 F

moi mon cœur qui bat.
be la vie en ro - se.

let's twist again

Words & Music by Kal Mann & Dave Appell

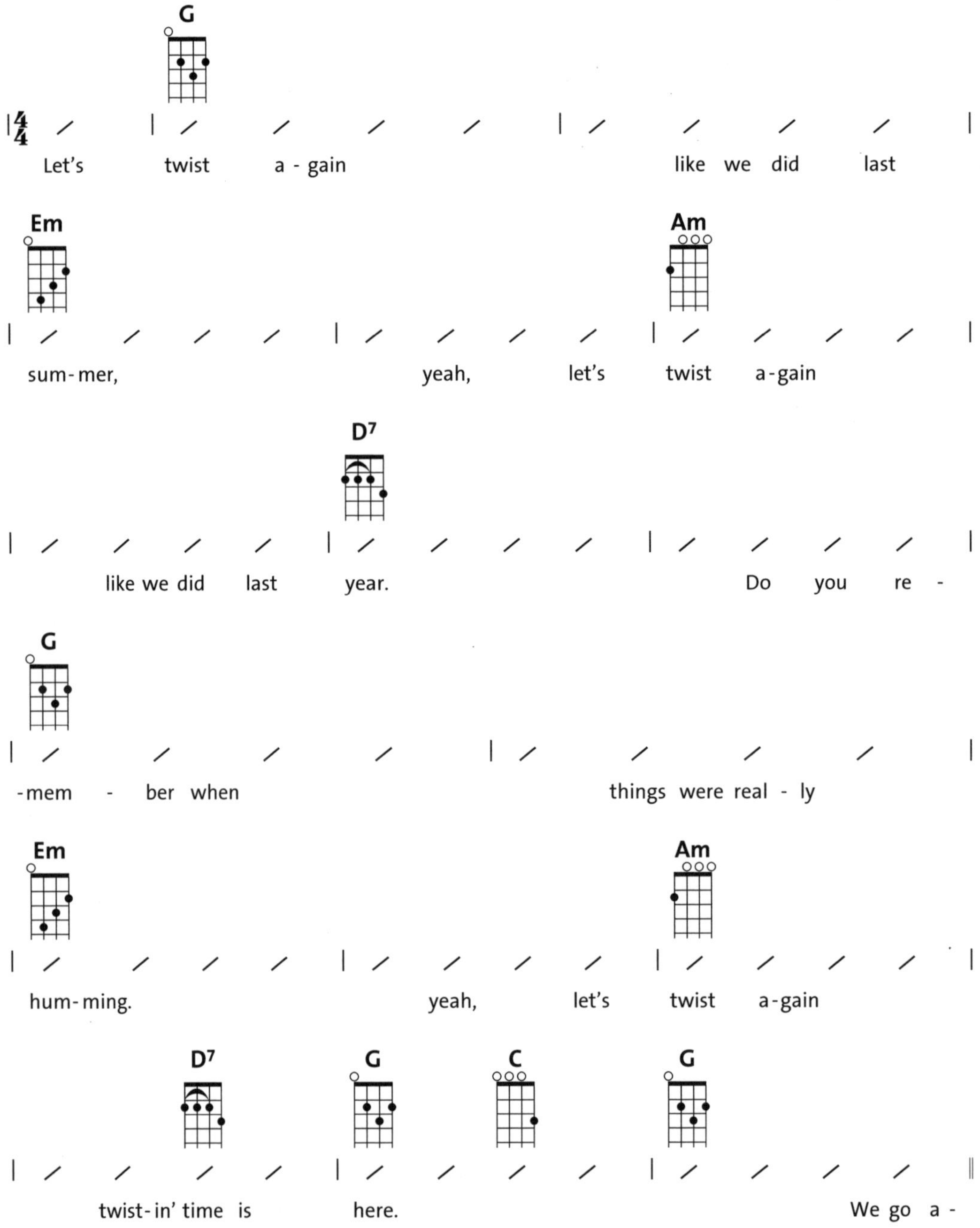

C G

round and a-round and a' up and down we go a -

C

- gain. Oh ba - by make me

D7

know you love me so and then let's

G Em

twist a-gain like we did last sum-mer.

Am

Yeah let's twist a - gain

D7 G C G

like we did last year.

life on mars?

Words & Music by David Bowie

4/4

F F/E F/E♭ D7
It's a God-aw-ful small af-fair to the girl with the mou - sy hair,

Gm Gm7 C7
but her mum-my is yell - ing 'no', and her dad-dy has told her to go.

F F/E F/E♭ Dsus4 D7
But her friend is no-where to be seen, now she walks through her sunk - en dream

Gm Gm7 C7
to the seat with the clear - est view, and she's hooked to the sil - ver screen.

A♭ Caug Fm A♭
But the film is a sad - dening bore, for she's lived it ten times or more.

poco rall.

D♭ Faug/A B♭m D♭7
She could spit in the eyes of fools as they ask her to fo - cus on

a tempo

B♭ E♭ Gm7 G♭aug

sail - lors fight-ing in the dance hall. Oh, man, look at those cave - men

F Fm Cm7 E♭m7

go. It's the frea - ki - est show. Take a look at the

B♭ E♭ Gm7 G♭aug

law - man beat-ing up the wrong guy. Oh, man, won-der if he'll ev - er know

F Fm Cm7 E♭m7

he's in the best sell-ing show. Is there life on

Gm Gm(maj7) Gm7 Gm6 F F♯dim

Mars?

Gm Ddim7 Am B♭ B♭m

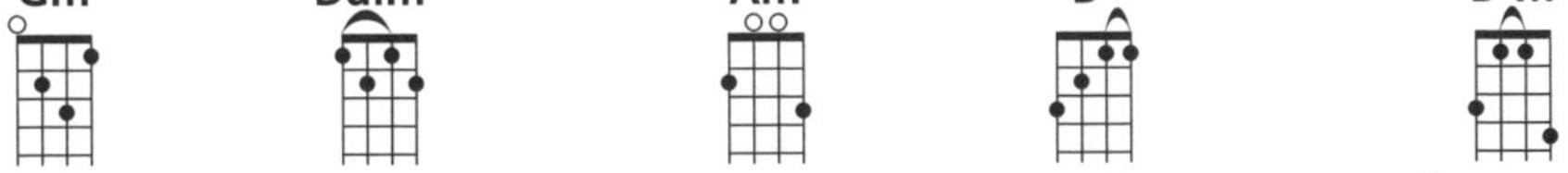

2/4 4/4

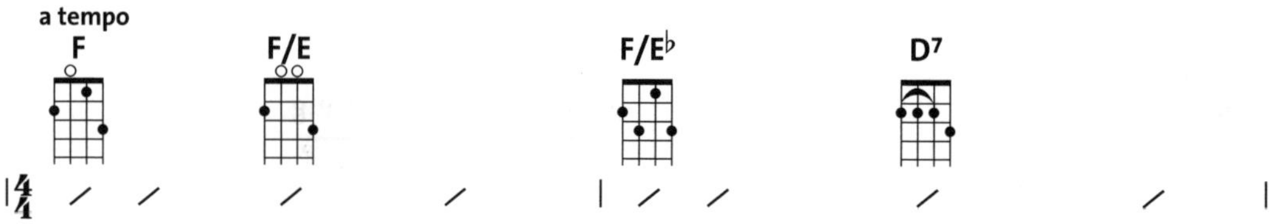

It's on A me ri-ca's tor-tured brow that Mick-ey Mouse has grown up a cow,

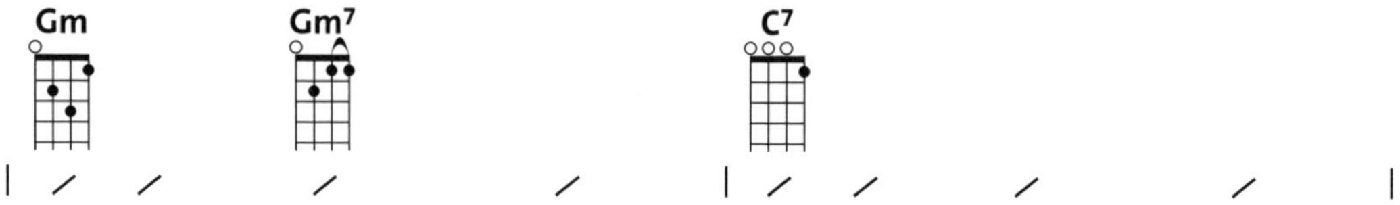

now the work-ers have struck for fame, 'cos Len-non's on sale a-gain.

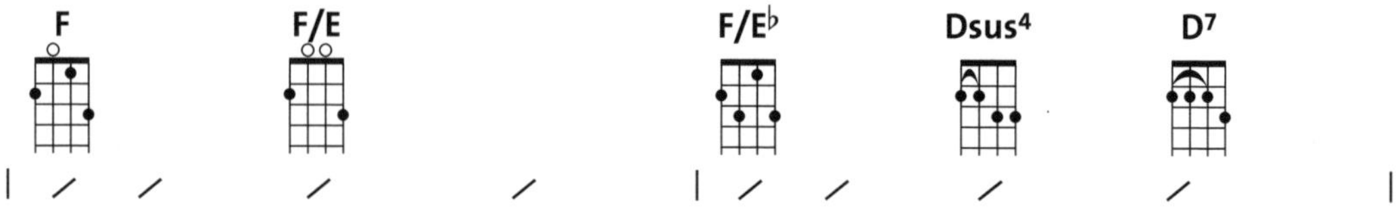

See the mice in their mil - lion hordes from I - bi - za to the Nor - folk Broads,

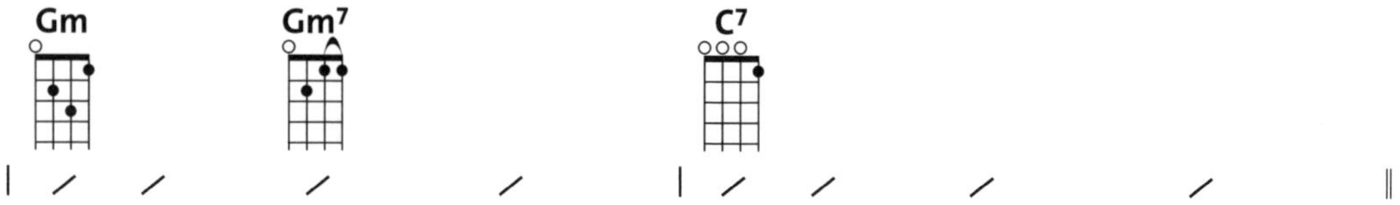

Rule Bri-tan-nia is out of bounds to my mo-ther, my dog and clowns.

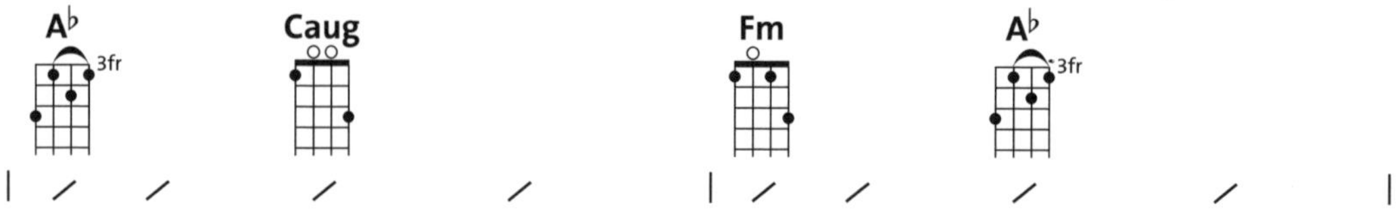

But the film is a sad - dening bore, 'cos I wrote it ten times or more,

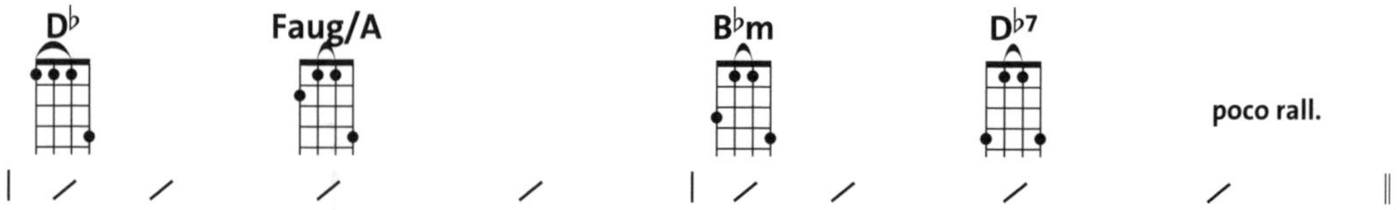

it's a-bout to be writ a-gain as I ask her to fo - cus on

a tempo

B♭ E♭ Gm7 G♭aug

sail - ors fight-ing in the dance hall. Oh, man, look at those cave - men

F Fm Cm7 E♭m7

go. It's the frea - ki - est show. Take a look at the

B♭ E♭ Gm7 G♭aug

law - man beat-ing up the wrong guy. Oh, man, won-der if he'll ev - er know

F Fm Cm7 E♭m7

he's in the best sell - ing show. Is there life on

Gm Gm(maj7) Gm7 Gm6 F F♯dim

Mars?

molto rall.

Gm B♭ E♭ E♭m B♭

love is all around

Words & Music by Reg Presley

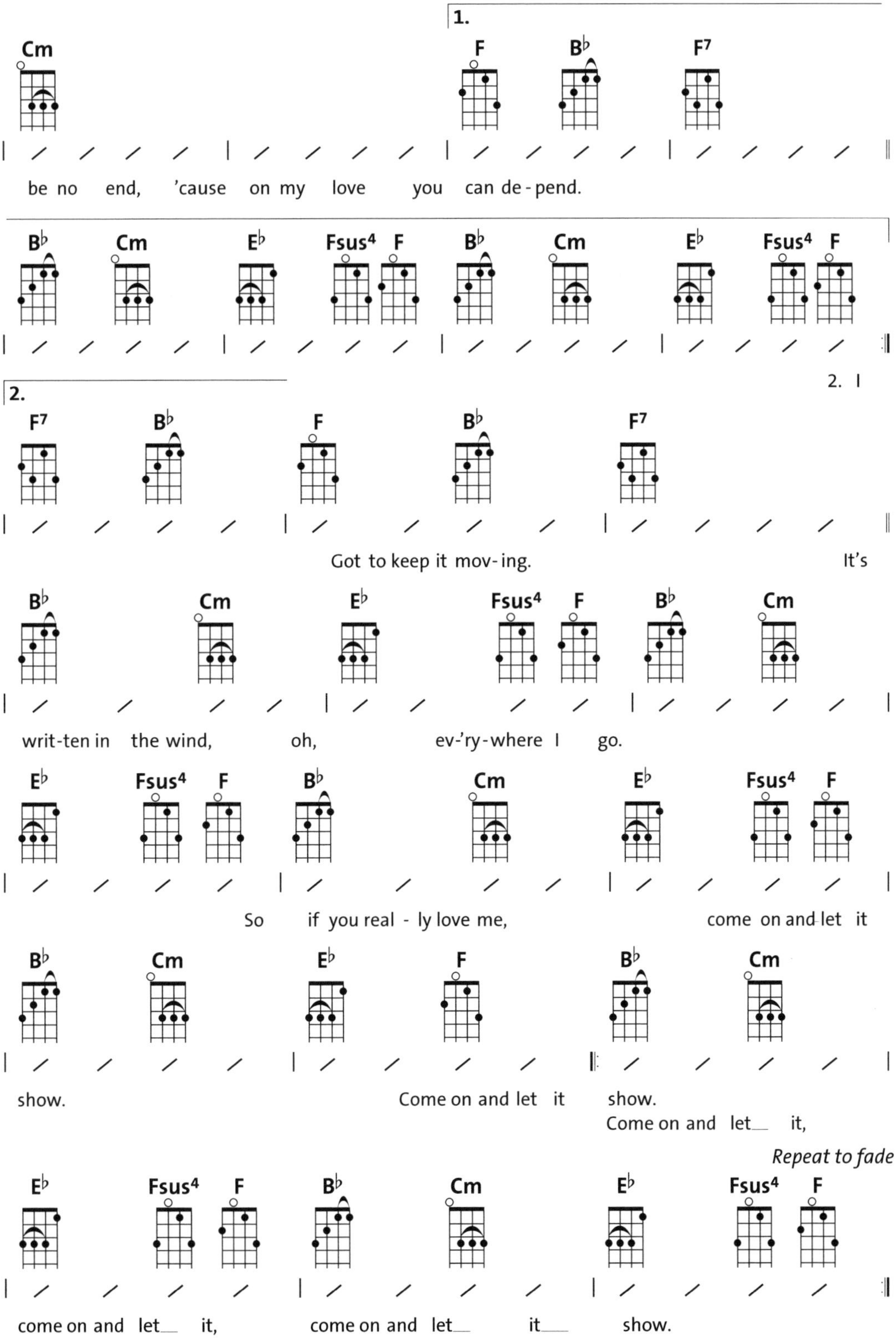
1.
Cm F B♭ F7
be no end, 'cause on my love you can de - pend.
B♭ Cm E♭ Fsus4 F B♭ Cm E♭ Fsus4 F
2. I
2.
F7 B♭ F B♭ F7
Got to keep it mov- ing. It's
B♭ Cm E♭ Fsus4 F B♭ Cm
writ-ten in the wind, oh, ev-'ry-where I go.
E♭ Fsus4 F B♭ Cm E♭ Fsus4 F
So if you real - ly love me, come on and let it
B♭ Cm E♭ F B♭ Cm
show. Come on and let it show.
Come on and let it,
Repeat to fade
E♭ Fsus4 F B♭ Cm E♭ Fsus4 F
come on and let it, come on and let it show.

sunny afternoon

Words & Music by Ray Davies

Dm | C7 | F

The tax - man's tak - en all my dough, And left me in my
girl - friend's gone off with my car, And gone back to her

C7 | A7 |

state - ly home: Laz - ing on a sun - ny af - ter - noon.
ma and pa; Tell - ing tales of drunk-en - ness and cruel-

Dm | C7 | F

And I can't sail my yacht, He's tak - en ev - 'ry
- ty Now I'm sit - ting here Sip - ping at my

C7 | A7 | | Dm

thing I've got All I've got's this sun-ny af - ter-noon.
ice - cold beer, Laz - ing on a sun-ny af - ter-noon.

| 𝄋 D7 | | G7

Save me, save me save me from this squeeze
Help me help me help me sail a - way,

C7 F

I've got a big fat mom-ma tryin' to break me.
You give me two good rea-sons why I ought to stay.

A7 Dm G9 Dm

And / 'Cause I love to live so pleas-ant - ly, live this life of lux-

G7 C7 F A7 Dm Dm7

- u - ry. Laz - ing on a sun-ny af-ter - noon.

Dm6 B♭ Dm A7 Dm Dm7

In sum-mer-time, In sum-mer-time,

D.S. al Coda

Dm6 B♭ Dm *To Coda* ⊕ 1. A7 2. A7

In sum-mer-time. My Ah

⊕ *Coda* A7 Dm Dm7 Dm6 B♭ Dm

In sum-mer-time. In sum-mer-time.

you never can tell

Words & Music by Chuck Berry

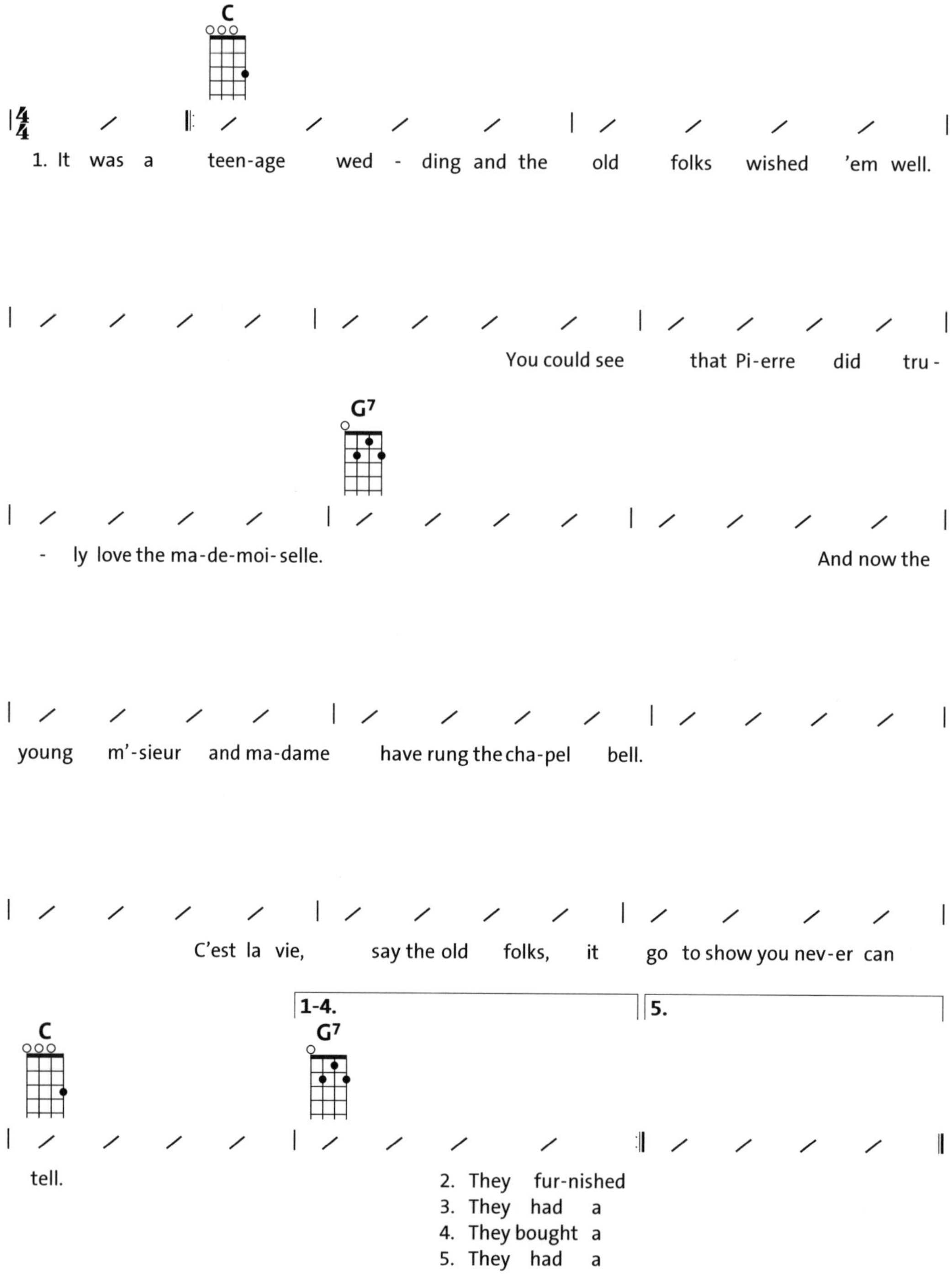

Verse 2:
They furnished up an apartment with a two-room Roebuck sale
The Coolerator was crammed with TV dinners and ginger ale
But when Pierre found work, the little monkey come in worked out well
C'est la vie, say the old folks, it go to show you never can tell.

Verse 3:
They had a hi-fi phono, boy did they let it blast
Seven hundred little records all rockin' rhythm and jazz
But when the sun went down the rapid tempo of the music fell
C'est la vie, say the old folks, it go to show you never can tell.

Verse 4:
They bought a souped-up Jitney was a cherry-red '53
And drove it down to Orleans to celebrate their anniversary
It was there that Pierre was waving to the lovely Mademoiselle
C'est la vie, say the old folks, it go to show you never can tell.

Verse 5:
They had a teenage wedding and the old folks wished them well
You could see that Pierre did truly love the Mademoiselle
And now the young M'sieur and Madame have rung the chapel bell
C'est la vie, say the old folks, it go to show you never can tell.

you really got me

Words & Music by Ray Davies

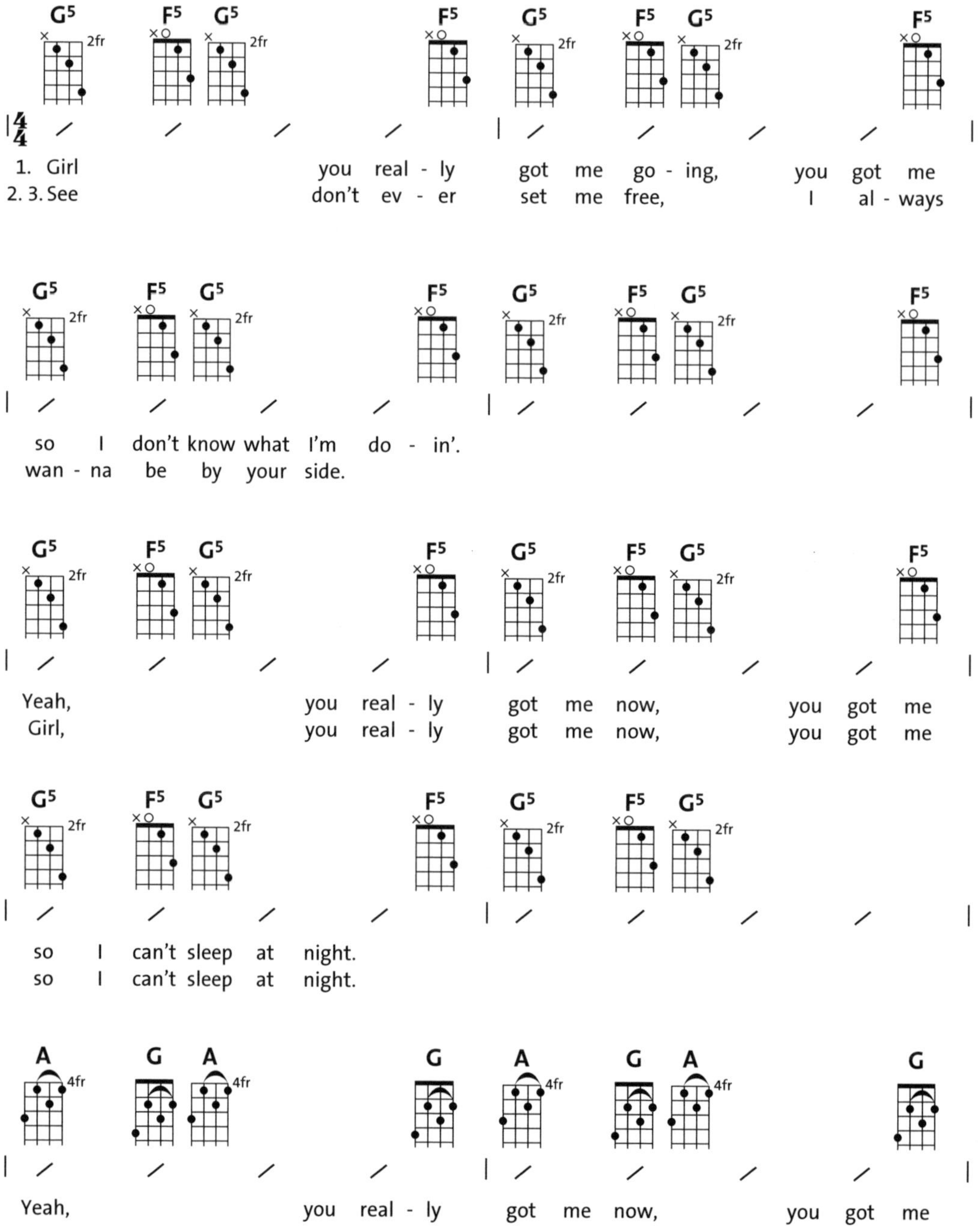

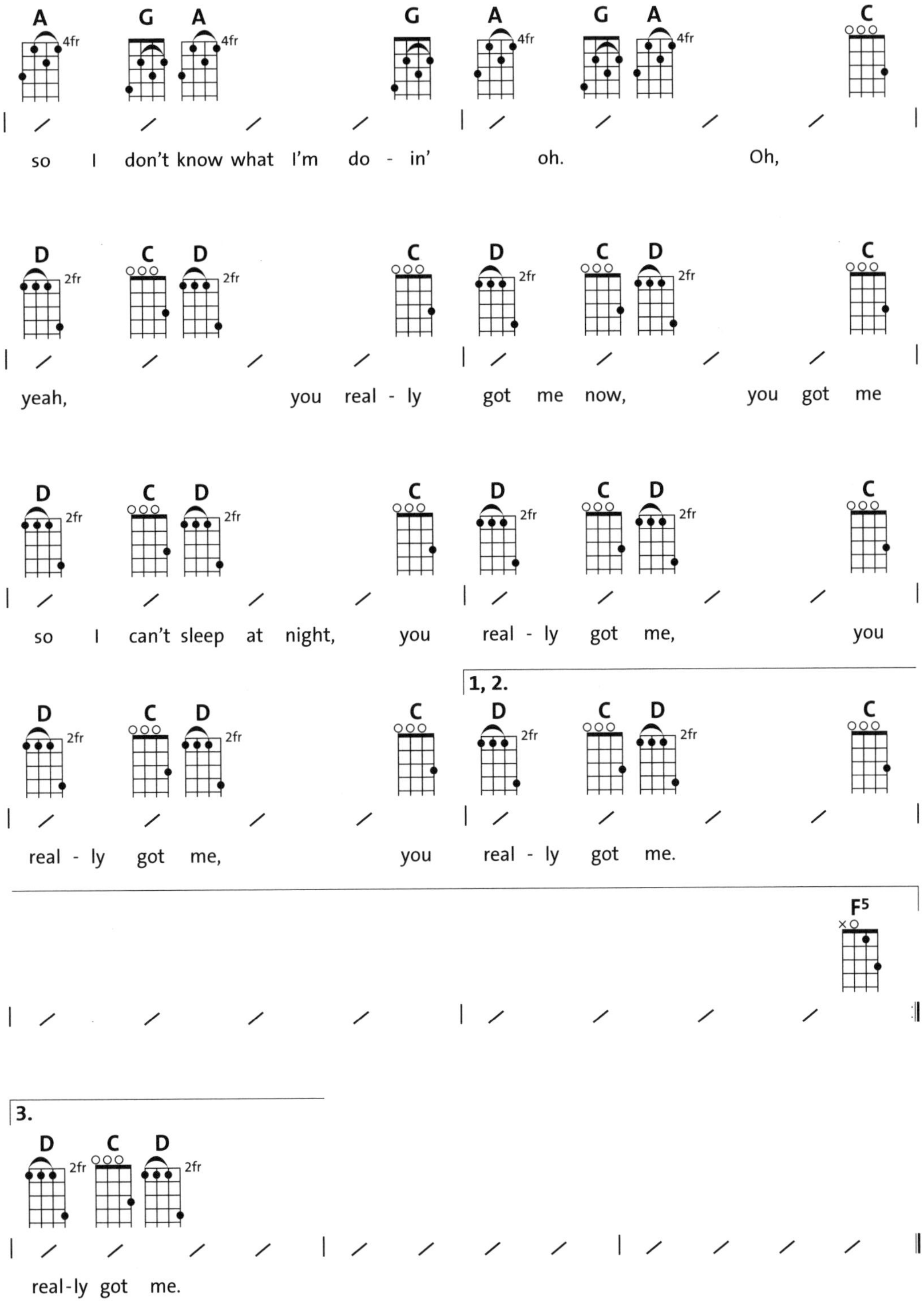
A G A G A G A C
so I don't know what I'm do - in' oh. Oh,
D C D C D C D C
yeah, you real - ly got me now, you got me
D C D C D C D C
so I can't sleep at night, you real - ly got me, you
D C D C
real - ly got me, you
1, 2.
D C D C
real - ly got me.
F5
3.
D C D
real-ly got me.

i say a little prayer

Words by Hal David
Music by Burt Bacharach

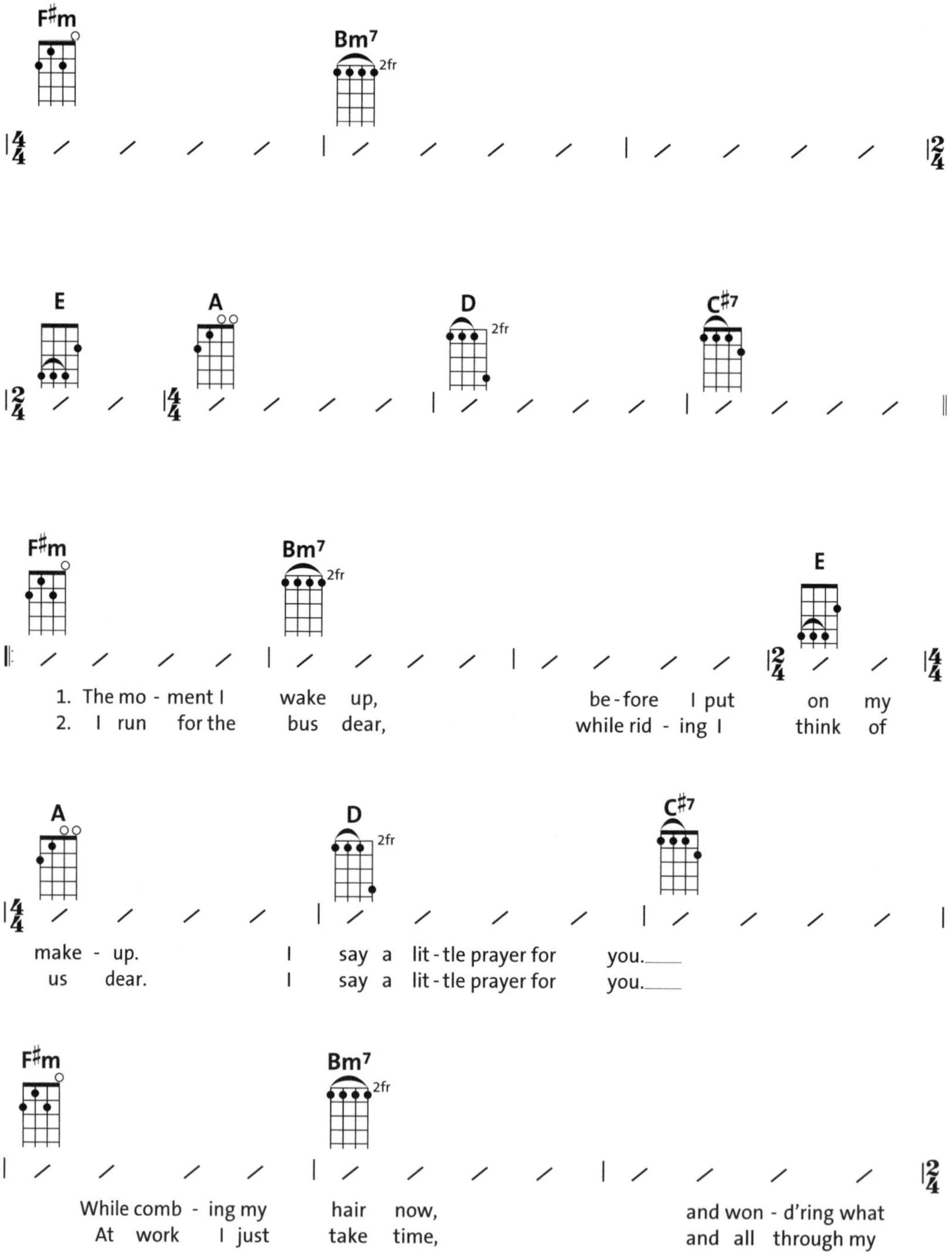

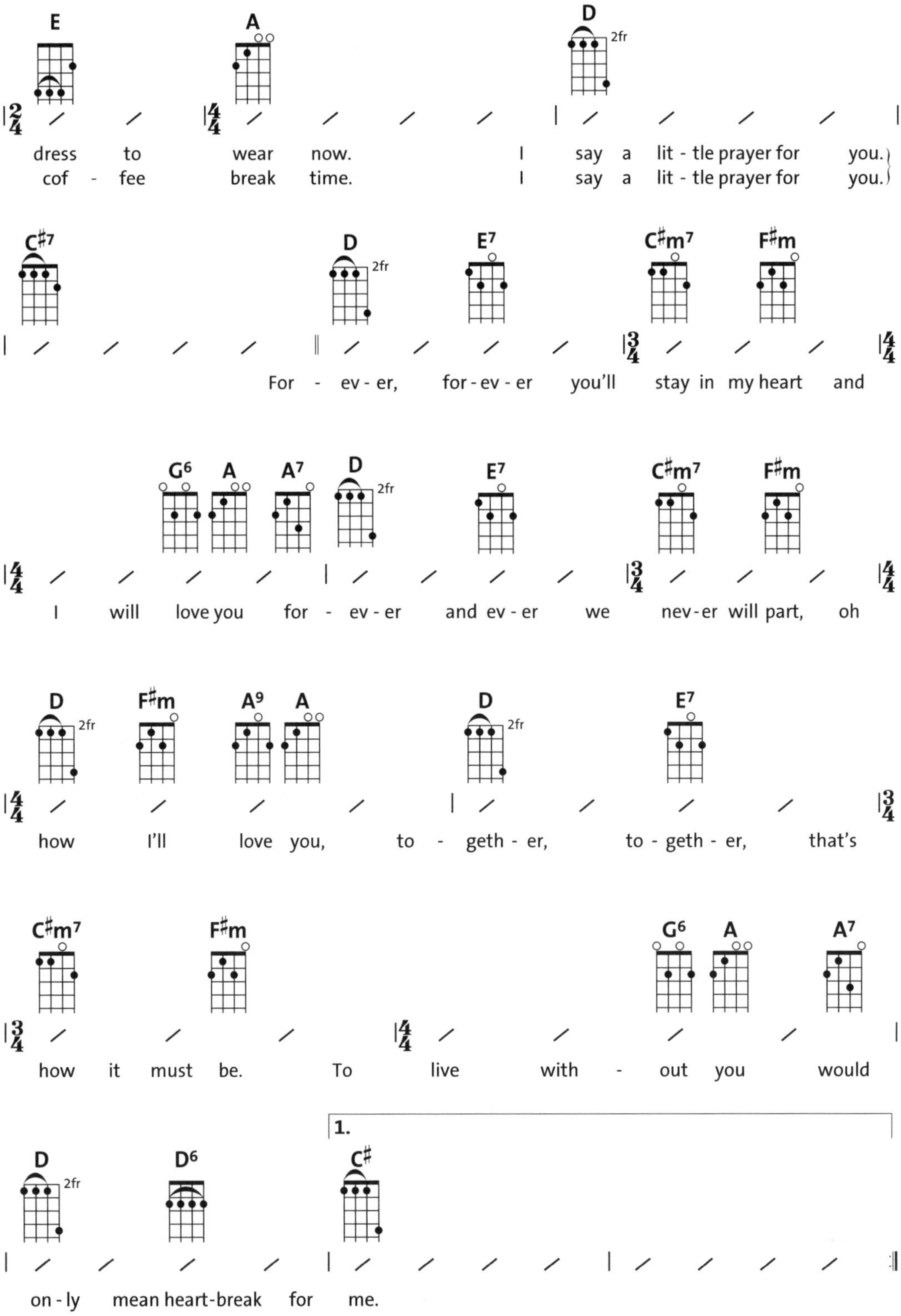
E A D
dress to wear now. I say a lit - tle prayer for you.
cof - fee break time. I say a lit - tle prayer for you.
C♯7 D E7 C♯m7 F♯m
For - ev - er, for - ev - er you'll stay in my heart and
G6 A A7 D E7 C♯m7 F♯m
I will love you for - ev - er and ev - er we nev - er will part, oh
D F♯m A9 A D E7
how I'll love you, to - geth - er, to - geth - er, that's
C♯m7 F♯m G6 A A7
how it must be. To live with - out you would
1.
D D6 C♯
on - ly mean heart - break for me.

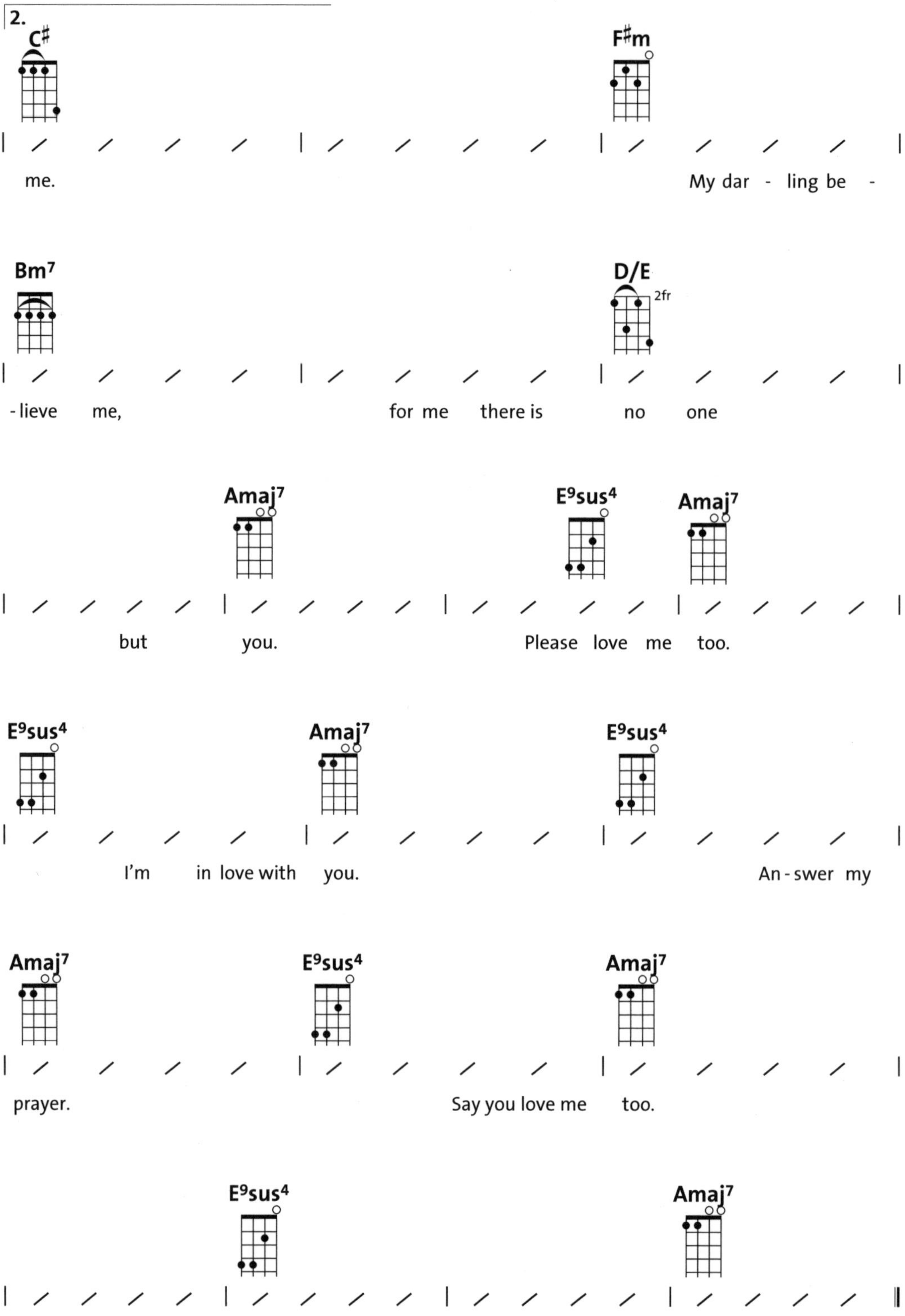

3 4 5 6 7 8
9/10(17545C